simone ♥ artist
linehan

IMAGES ARE PHOTOGRAPHED BY ARTIST SIMONE LINEHAN
FROM HER EVERYDAY MEALS, DINING OUT EXPERIENCES, BREAKY IN BED,
CAMP COOK UPS AND NUTRITIOUS FOOD WITH LOVED ONES.

Food glorious food!

From dining out, to camp cook ups, to breaky in bed and the humble steamed veg...
but really... it's all about the glorious colours!

As artists we love to unpack visual life in front of us exploring the individual elements.

We are constantly pursuing colour and value combinations to create a particular mood or feeling within our work.

I'm sharing this book with you as a small insight to how I simplify the colours around us and see the beauty in the food I eat.

Enjoy!

COLLECT THE SET!
CHECK OUT **BOOKS 1+2** & OTHERS IN THE COLLECTION

COLOUR INSPIRATIONS #001

COLOUR INSPIRATIONS #002

COLOUR INSPIRATIONS #003

COLOUR INSPIRATIONS #004

COLOUR INSPIRATIONS #005

COLOUR INSPIRATIONS #006

COLOUR INSPIRATIONS #007

COLOUR INSPIRATIONS #008

COLOUR INSPIRATIONS #009

COLOUR INSPIRATIONS #010

COLOUR INSPIRATIONS #011

COLOUR INSPIRATIONS #012

COLOUR INSPIRATIONS #013

COLOUR INSPIRATIONS #014

COLOUR INSPIRATIONS #015

COLOUR INSPIRATIONS #016

COLOUR INSPIRATIONS #017

COLOUR INSPIRATIONS #018

COLOUR INSPIRATIONS #019

COLOUR INSPIRATIONS #020

COLOUR INSPIRATIONS #021

COLOUR INSPIRATIONS #022

COLOUR INSPIRATIONS #023

COLOUR INSPIRATIONS #024

COLOUR INSPIRATIONS #025

COLOUR INSPIRATIONS #026

COLOUR INSPIRATIONS #027

COLOUR INSPIRATIONS #028

COLOUR INSPIRATIONS #029

COLOUR INSPIRATIONS #030

COLOUR INSPIRATIONS #031

COLOUR INSPIRATIONS #032

COLOUR INSPIRATIONS #033

COLOUR INSPIRATIONS #034

COLOUR INSPIRATIONS #035

COLOUR INSPIRATIONS #036

COLOUR INSPIRATIONS #037

COLOUR INSPIRATIONS #038

COLOUR INSPIRATIONS #039

COLOUR INSPIRATIONS #040

COLOUR INSPIRATIONS #041

COLOUR INSPIRATIONS #042

COLOUR INSPIRATIONS #043

COLOUR INSPIRATIONS #044

COLOUR INSPIRATIONS #045

COLOUR INSPIRATIONS #046

COLOUR INSPIRATIONS #047

COLOUR INSPIRATIONS #048

COLOUR INSPIRATIONS #050

COLOUR INSPIRATIONS #051

COLOUR INSPIRATIONS #052

COLOUR INSPIRATIONS #053

COLOUR INSPIRATIONS #049

COLOUR INSPIRATIONS #054

COLOUR INSPIRATIONS #055

COLOUR INSPIRATIONS #056

COLOUR INSPIRATIONS #057

COLOUR INSPIRATIONS #058

COLOUR INSPIRATIONS #059

COLOUR INSPIRATIONS #060

THE COLOUR WHEEL - 'DECONSTRUCTED'

PRIMARY COLORS

Red, Yellow and Blue are the primary colors. These are the three basic colors that are used to mix all hues.

1 red PRIMARY

1 yellow PRIMARY

1 blue PRIMARY

SECONDARY COLORS

Orange, Green and Purple are the secondary colors. They are achieved by mixing two primary colors together.

2 orange SECONDARY

2 purple SECONDARY

2 green SECONDARY

3 red orange TERTIARY

3 red purple TERTIARY

TERTIARY COLORS

Tertiary colors are more subtle hues which are achieved by mixing a primary and a secondary color that are adjacent on the color wheel.

3 yellow orange TERTIARY

3 blue purple TERTIARY

3 yellow green TERTIARY

3 blue green TERTIARY

MONOCHROME

Monochromatic colour schemes are derived from a single base hue (colour) and extended using its shades, tones and tints.

You can use ANY colour (and variations of it) for this theory.

COMPLEMENTARY / OPPOSITE / CONTRASTING

A pair, including a primary and secondary colour, on opposite sides of the colour wheel.

- RED + GREEN
- BLUE + ORANGE
- YELLOW + PURPLE

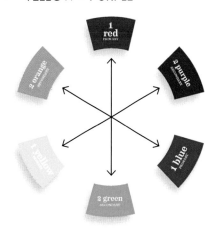

ANALOGOUS
Analogous colours are groups of three (or so) colours that are next to each other on the colour wheel.
It may be a primary, a secondary and a tertiary.

They produce a calming affect.

IE: Red, orange and red-orange or blue, green and green-blue etc

LOW INTENSITY
Low intensity colours are mixed by using opposites/complementary/contrasting colours together.
IE: RED & GREEN
BLUE & ORANGE
YELLOW & PURPLE

A different percentage of each colour produces earthy / muddier colours.

ONE EXAMPLE WITH TWO COMPLEMENTARY COLOURS:
Starting with BLUE mix in a small amount of ORANGE you produce a DEEP NAVY.

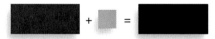

Yet if you begin with ORANGE and add some BLUE you will mix a BROWNY colour.

Not to confuse you, but we also have a range of cool primaries and warm primaries!

It's wonderful information as once you get the hang of mixing your colours (primary to secondary and so on) then you can experiment with just using the cool range and warm range to produce different ranges of colours.

Within each primary colour you can have warms and cools.

We have warm blues and cool blues, warm reds, cool reds and warm yellows and cool yellows.

A **warm** blue would have a red bias (reddish blue) since red is a warm colour.

A **cool** blue would have a green bias (greenish blue) since green is a cool colour.

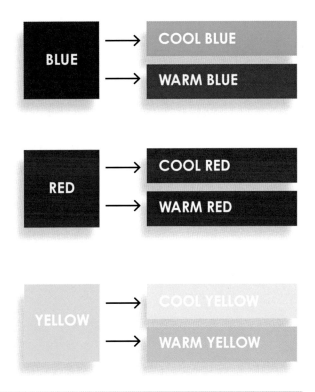

want much brighter colours in your colour wheel mixing?

If you want clean, comtemporary colours swap red for **magenta** and blue for **turquoise** then mix as usual.

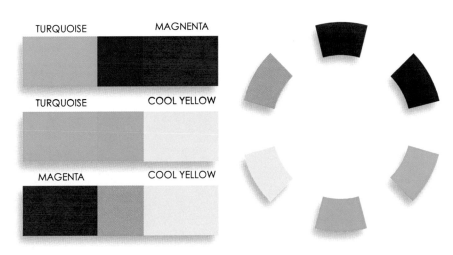

PRIMARIES - COOL AND WARM - MIXING

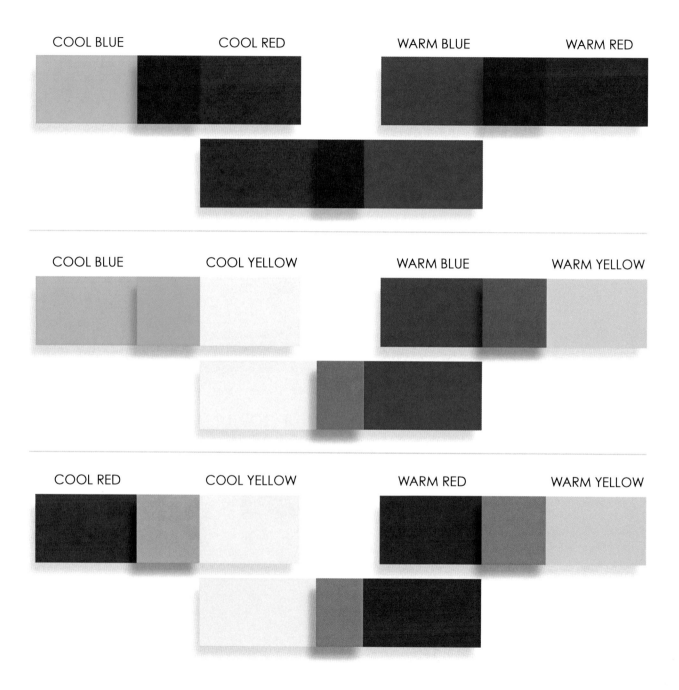

COOL BLUE   COOL RED   WARM BLUE   WARM RED

COOL BLUE   COOL YELLOW   WARM BLUE   WARM YELLOW

COOL RED   COOL YELLOW   WARM RED   WARM YELLOW

COLOUR INSPIRATIONS #013

BE INSPIRED BY THE
COLOUR PALETTES
FOR YOUR NEXT
CREATIVE PROJECT

© ORIGINAL ARTWORK BY SIMONE LINEHAN

simone ♥ artist
linehan

COLOUR INSPIRATIONS #029

USE ALL OR JUST
SOME OF THE
COLOURS PLUS
ADD SOME EXTRAS

© ORIGINAL ARTWORK BY SIMONE LINEHAN

simone
linehan artist

Made in United States
Orlando, FL
09 December 2024

55261646R00040